Is Your Business a Prison?

The keys to unlocking entrepreneurial freedom and growing a fulfilling business you love: a guidebook for heart-centred women

Chenae Carey

This book is dedicated to you.
It takes courage, determination and grit to start a business.

Contents

Introduction

Chapter 1: Overwhelm

Is Overwhelm Your Primary Business Prison? 15

Chapter 2: Low Self-Esteem

Is Low Self-Esteem Your Primary Business Prison? 27

Chapter 3: All The Things

Is Doing 'All The Things' Your Primary Business Prison? 35

Chapter 4: Who To Trust

Is Knowing Who To Trust Your Primary Business Prison?......45

Chapter 5: Comfort Zone

Is Staying In Your Comfort Zone Your Primary Business Prison? 55

Chapter 6: Fierce Independence

Is Your Fierce Independence Your Primary Business Prison?... 67

Where To From Here?

About the Author 81

Introduction

Your business has become a prison and you don't even realise it. What's worse is that it's a prison of your own making.

My guess is that you started a business to give yourself more freedom. You wanted a certain kind of lifestyle - you didn't want to have to report to a boss or a manager. You wanted flexibility - you wanted to choose your own hours and the clients you work with. You wanted to set your own availability, take time off over school holidays, and spend time with your family without having to ask anyone else's permission. You wanted to be able to easily attend school events, be there for your kids... or your dogs... or your plants. You wanted the ability to spend as much time as possible doing what lights you up.

You started your business to feel free.

So, this business you created to give yourself more freedom, *how's that going*?

Do you *feel* free?

Or does your business feel like a prison?

It can be hard to tell at a glance, especially because many heart-centred women love to convince themselves everything is just fine. We can tend to put ourselves last or mask what's really going on, not wanting to be a burden. It takes a practical measurement to actually see it.

Here's a temperature check. See how many of these answers make you feel trapped:

Are you working longer hours than you did in your traditional job?

How late do you work at night?

Can you attend school assembly if your child receives an award?

Do you feel chained to your desk?

Are you working the hours you thought you would be?

Do you feel guilty for working when you'd like to be with your family?

When was the last time you took a day off?

Is your family lucky to see you emerge from your office before 7pm?

Can your business afford for you to take a holiday?

Does your business contribute meaningfully to the household income?

Would your business come to a grinding halt if you took a break?

Perhaps you're missing those important school events you promised you'd be at and you feel frustrated that you're not being the mum you want to be. Maybe you feel guilty for not being present as a partner or seeing your friends and family as much as you would like. Generally, the whole working for yourself thing has not gone as planned.

If you have ever found yourself working on the couch late at night or glued to your device all day long, ignoring everyone around you and neglecting your home, doing things that *just need to get done,* then there is a good chance I can help. This book is for anyone whose business hasn't given them the freedom that they were seeking when they left their regular work behind.

In the following pages, you'll find a guided journey designed to help you unlock your entrepreneurial freedom. But if it's going to work, you'll need to do this one little thing for yourself... Commit to it.

HI, I'M CHENAE

In case we haven't yet met, I'm Chenae and I've been an entrepreneur and business owner since I was in my late twenties. I've had the pleasure of working with many women-led businesses in my entrepreneurial journey, and one thing I've noticed is that we, as women, sabotage our business growth by getting in our own way. I've come across a gamut of subconscious beliefs and fears (I call them prisons) and I've discovered that these prisons don't discriminate. I've seen them in every industry

I've worked with, including health and wellness, coaching, spirituality, counselling, healing therapies and business support to name a few. After working together, the women I have coached enjoy more clients, more time and ultimately more freedom in their businesses and I want that for you.

HOW TO USE THIS BOOK

I've written *Is Your Business a Prison?* as a guidebook, designed to take you on an intentional journey to explore some of the prisons I see trapping women in business. You get to peek behind the curtains as I share some juicy client stories so you can see how these prisons show up. I'll provide you with reflective practices to help you understand the depth and impact of these prisons and how to free yourself. With that in mind, here is what I recommend you do to get the most out of this book.

1. Read when you won't be disturbed

2. Keep your journal and pen handy

3. Take notes in *one* place, and avoid chopping and changing

4. Complete every activity and don't skip any just because they feel hard

5. If you feel like skipping an exercise, examine why and be honest with yourself

6. Allow time to reflect and journal after each chapter

7. Debrief with your entrepreneurial friends

8. Share your insights online and tag me so I know which chapter you're on

Each chapter includes an audio practice for you to do. You'll find them all at www.chenaecarey.com/bookresources. The password you need is FREEDOM (all uppercase). To share your insights with me, you can catch me online at @chenaecareycoaching on Facebook or @chenaecarey on Instagram. Send me a message. I'd love to hear from you!

GETTING THE MOST OUT OF THIS BOOK

This book will give you freedom if you give it the energy, time and attention it deserves. I want you to get as much as possible out of this book, but nobody can do the work for you.

To use this book as intended, commit to making time for self-reflection and journaling as you read. Set yourself up for success by actually listening to the guided meditations or visualisations, and doing so when you can be fully present and won't be disturbed. Be a diligent student who completes every practice. Having a business is a freedom not afforded to all, and what I need from you is recognition. I need you to recognise your privilege. Do not squander this precious opportunity. If you cannot commit right now, put this book down until you can. What I'm saying is - and I say this with love - don't bother reading if you're going to half-arse it.

If you're ready and willing to give it your best, for yourself and your business...

If you're ready to claim the keys to your freedom...

If you're ready to inject fun, excitement and joy back into your business...

If you're ready to do this for those who can't...

Grab your journal and favourite pen and let's begin.

WHAT IS FREEDOM?

Let's explore this idea of freedom and why it matters to so many entrepreneurs. Freedom comes in many forms. We can have financial freedom, emotional freedom, physical freedom, location independence and so on. If you're reading this, there is a damn good chance that no matter how long ago you started your business, you did so because you yearned for the freedom that having a business can offer. You know exactly what I'm talking about, don't you? The excitement of having flexibility. The strong desire to make choices you wouldn't otherwise get to make in a job. The yearning to be in charge of your schedule. The dream of doing things *your* way, free from limitations and restrictions.

I call this *entrepreneurial freedom.*

I believe that it is entirely possible (for those of us who are privileged enough to have businesses) to pursue freedom right now. And I believe we *should.* I also believe that the pursuit of freedom should be at the forefront of our focus as entrepreneurs. Chasing our desires, pursuing richness and depth with a sense of freedom in our hearts and minds.

I love this quote from John O'Donohue because it really gets me thinking. I pause and consider what freedom might feel like in my later years and it's *exciting.* My mind begins to imagine what our experiences of freedom in old age would be like if we actively pursued freedom *now.* I don't know about you, but that thought sends tingles down my spine.

Freedom can be one of the wonderful fruits of old age.

To pursue freedom, we need to understand what it means to us. I think it's fair to assume that we each define freedom differently because what excites and motivates you might feel dull, scary or even overwhelming to someone else. Regardless of how you perceive freedom, there is no doubt that you started a business with entrepreneurial freedom in mind.

Like all freedoms, entrepreneurial freedom means something different to each of us so let's begin by exploring what entrepreneurial freedom means to you.

ACTIVITY: WHAT IS ENTREPRENEURIAL FREEDOM?

This activity is designed to illuminate what entrepreneurial freedom means to you. Grab a journal and pen plus something you can use to set a timer, like your phone or smartwatch.

1. Open your journal to a blank page

2. Write the date at the top

3. Write this heading: ENTREPRENEURIAL FREEDOM

4. Set a timer for 5 minutes

5. Write down as many different types of entrepreneurial freedom as you can - e.g. working from anywhere, choosing my work hours, setting my own prices, doing rewarding work etc.

When the timer goes off, look at what you've written and rate them in order of importance to you, starting with the most critical aspect of entrepreneurial freedom at #1. Once you've done that, pause for a moment to look at what you've written. This is what *motivates* you, what drives you. If you're not experiencing enough of these things, your business probably feels like a prison.

Here are some of the things on my list from when I did this exercise myself:

1. Choosing my own hours

2. Using my spirituality and intuition in my work

3. Not having a boss

4. Doing work that I love

5. Work that fulfils me

6. Being able to go to yoga during business hours

7. Working from home with my fur baby

8. Not having to ask permission for time off

9. Making a difference in the way I want

10. Not commuting in traffic

11. Working with and hiring like-minded women

12. Supporting other small businesses

13. Going to the supermarket in the middle of the day

14. Being able to work from anywhere

15. Booking self-care appointments during business hours

16. Contribute to my household income with work that doesn't drain me

WHERE IT ALL BEGAN

When my role at my day job was discontinued, my business was still a side hustle. Taking redundancy was an opportunity to turn my business into my main income stream, so I did it. The yearning for the freedoms on my list above kept me focused and determined to create a business that supported a lifestyle that I loved.

Nowadays, when I'm not getting enough of these freedoms in my life, I feel frustrated, overwhelmed and burdened. I can be a total pain in the arse and I'm no fun to be around. My business doesn't get the energy and attention it deserves to function optimally. Knowing and living my personal list of freedoms is vital!

Luckily, it's a rare occurrence that I don't prioritise my freedoms. If there is a deficit, I course-correct quickly. That's how I know how to support you to do the same. In this book, I show you what I do so that you too can create and prioritise your entrepreneurial freedom.

Now that you have an idea of what entrepreneurial freedom means to you and where there are deficits of freedom, let's talk about what's getting in the way.

NEGATIVE SUBCONSCIOUS BELIEFS

Your subconscious beliefs determine everything in your life and business. This includes the quality and quantity of your entrepreneurial freedom, or lack thereof. If you are not experiencing that liberating sense of freedom that motivated you to start your business in the first place, your negative subconscious beliefs are likely getting in the way. Negative subconscious beliefs dictate your experience of entrepreneurial freedom.

> *"The longest and most exciting journey is the journey inwards."*
>
> STANISLAVSKI,
> RUSSIAN DRAMATIST
> AND THINKER

So what is a subconscious belief?

To understand subconscious beliefs, we need to discuss two key aspects of our consciousness that my mentor and Principal of the Institute for Intuitive Intelligence Dr Ricci-Jane Adams outlines in her book *Spiritually Fierce*. Our conscious reasoning mind is our personality, our likes and dislikes. We like to think that this part of us is in charge, but it's not. The subconscious makes up 90-95% of our consciousness, and as the name suggests, the subconscious operates below our conscious reasoning mind. As we go about our lives, the beliefs (both positive and negative) stored in our subconscious inform our experiences and reality. I'm most interested in the negative beliefs we have stored in our subconscious because those negative beliefs can turn your business into a prison.

You may already be familiar with subconscious beliefs. If you are, what do you do with your negative beliefs? Do you go about your business avoiding them? Or do you explore the contents of your subconscious and clear out the negative ones? Meeting and transmuting our negative subconscious beliefs (aka our fears) takes courage, willingness and effort. As a result, many of us simply avoid this deep work, privileging our comfort zones and wondering why our lives and businesses lack creativity and growth. Author John O'Donohue suggests that it is a courageous person who can identify their fears and work with them as forces of creativity and growth.

Just as there's more than one type of freedom, there are also many different entrepreneurial prisons. Each subconscious belief is like a prison; they keep us locked up, unable to experience or enjoy the entrepreneurial freedoms that motivated us to go into business for ourselves.

I've come across a gamut of subconscious beliefs and fears, what I call prisons, in my entrepreneurial journey. So I've put together a list of beliefs stored in the subconscious of many business owners and some examples of how they can show up.

I'm not good enough

She is constantly sitting idle, distracting herself, avoiding marketing and promotion for her business. Stuck in inaction, she's afraid she hasn't got what it takes to create, grow or expand her business.

I have to work hard to succeed

She is busting her ass, often working hard for very little, working long hours, late into the night, prioritising tasks that aren't important so she feels forever busy. She grew up watching adults pride themselves on working hard. She feels proud of being a battler, being the underdog.

Is Your Business a Prison?

I don't know what I'm doing

She believes the thoughts that tell her she's stupid, silly, not smart enough. She experiences constant negative mind chatter about having no idea what she's doing, that she shouldn't even bother. Her confidence wavers and she doesn't believe in herself.

If I succeed, I'll lose everything

She's addicted to her comfort zone, even if it's shit and she's miserable. She feels deeply unfulfilled in her personal life, but she keeps her business small because too much success means she won't need her husband anymore. If she's honest with herself, nothing is working but she's terrified to take a risk in case everything crumbles. It might be the best thing that could ever happen for her, but she's too scared to try.

I am alone

She feels as though she is the only one experiencing what she's going through, that nobody understands her business struggles and challenges. She feels unsupported and like she's carrying a heavy burden upon her shoulders that nobody can assist her with. She feels like a victim of her circumstances.

I don't deserve abundance

She tells herself she's terrible with money. She brings money in and almost immediately it's gone. She is frugal with her money. Being generous feels scary. She heavily discounts her work because she's afraid nobody will buy from her.

I am unworthy of success

She is crippled by her feelings of unworthiness. She rejects compliments and doesn't allow people to help her. She doesn't feel worthy to receive any kind of help and insists on doing everything herself. The idea of outsourcing is mind-boggling to her. The success of others makes her feel jealous.

I don't trust myself

She likes to feel in control. Her business keeps her so busy that she sabotages her ability to enjoy life. She makes decisions from her head and ignores her heart. She has inconsistent income. Making a sale is exciting, but she sabotages it soon enough. She swings from being flippant to micro-managing things.

I am insignificant

She feels small and unseen. Self-promotion is her worst nightmare. The idea of getting on camera terrifies her. Marketing feels painfully uncomfortable. She compares herself to the big personalities in her life and says mean things to herself. She doesn't often speak up or speak out.

I can't trust others

She has been burned, so she is wary of almost everyone, making it hard to connect with others. She's overworked and always tired because she doesn't trust anyone else with her business. It impacts her relationships with clients, suppliers, other business owners and communities. She is misunderstood, appearing standoffish in her efforts to protect herself.

That's quite a list! And even though this list is not exhaustive, there is a good chance you can see yourself in at least some of these fears, if not all!

ACTIVITY: GRAB YOUR JOURNAL

Grab your journal and read through the list of beliefs again, writing down the ones that resonate. Awareness is the first step, so for bonus points write down how each belief shows up for you and how they make your business feel like a prison.

WHICH PRISON ARE YOU IN?

We're going to explore six of the above prisons together. I've selected the ones that I see the most in my work. As you read through each prison and complete each practice, there's a pretty good chance that you will see yourself in at least one, if not more, of the prisoner stories. I wouldn't be surprised if you see yourself in them all, even if only in a small way. That's why this book exists.

WHERE ARE THE KEYS?

You might be wondering: *if I am in a prison, how do I get myself out?* This is a great question. By the time you reach the keys that I share at the end of each chapter, you'll likely have some ideas on what you can do to free yourself. You'll see what my clients (aka former prisoners) have done and the results they've achieved.

Like any prison, yours is made up of individual jail cells. Our subconscious beliefs have layers, so not only is your prison made up of a number of different cells, each cell requires a specific key. While there are common patterns within our fears, you are unique, and so is the set of keys that will set you free. In many instances, you'll need a combination of keys. Just like you see during a jail-break in the movies, a prisoner has to get through a whole bunch of different doors and try a number of different tactics before they reach freedom.

> *"The only real prison is fear, and the only real freedom is from fear."*
>
> AUNG SAN SUU KYI

Each of the six prisons in this book includes a list of keys. The keys are actions to help you unlock each layer (cell). There are many keys because we are all unique, which means the lock on each cell is unique. Some of your prison cells will unlock when you implement something practical, while others might need a combination, perhaps some energy work, a change of perspective or some external input. Please don't expect that only one key is required for one prison. A better way to look at it is that there is one key for each cell, and by the end, you'll have a bunch of keys (actions) on a chain.

You unlock a cell by taking action. The freedom you yearn for requires work. If it didn't, it would all be working out for you right now. We now understand that:

Prisons = negative subconscious beliefs

Keys = actions

If you're ready to collect the keys and break free, let's take a look at the first prison.

Chapter 1: Overwhelm
IS OVERWHELM YOUR PRIMARY BUSINESS PRISON?

Your overwhelm is the result of either a lack of discipline, shitty boundaries, or both. There, I said it. With that uncomfortable reality out of the way, let's see what it looks like. For one, you likely work later or longer than you'd like, and while you're incredibly competent and can handle variety, you're overcommitted. You are barely surviving, let alone thriving, and it's become so normal you don't even realise you're living inside a prison of your own making. The trouble is you feel important when you are busy.

Here are some examples of how this prison shows up:

- Your to-do list is so long it feels like you'll never accomplish anything

- You don't like to ask for help when you can do it yourself

- It's hard to admit you've bitten off more than you can chew

- You enjoy being needed, wanted or relied upon

- If you step away, you're worried your business will come to a grinding halt

- You rarely get to bed as early as you'd like

- You're so generous that you spend longer than you should on calls/ sessions, which makes you run late, adding to your overwhelm

- When on the couch with your family at night, you're physically present but distracted by your phone/laptop/tablet

- You like to be reliable, often to your own detriment

- People often expect you to be busy, late or RSVP with 'not attending'

Negative subconscious beliefs associated with this prison

- I have to work hard to succeed
- I'm not good enough
- I am alone
- When I give all of me, I am more valuable
- I don't deserve abundance
- I can't trust others
- Asking for help makes me weak
- I can only rely on myself
- If I don't do it, nobody else will
- I enjoy feeling important and busy
- I can't have it all

Prisoner story: Hannah the Health Practitioner

When we first started working together, Hannah was burning the candle at both ends, overwhelmed and trapped inside a prison of her overcommitment. An intelligent, educated, loyal, generous and skilled multitasker, her generosity and juggling had snowballed, leaving her no time for rest and downtime, and very little time with her family.

Running two businesses meant that she was never short of tasks, so she was so accustomed to feeling overwhelmed that she prioritised everything. She enjoyed being dynamic, but was totally overcommitted. That meant her relaxation time and family time ended up being neglected. Austrian poet and novelist Rilke said that difficulty is one of the greatest friends of the soul, but Hannah had gone too far, beyond difficulties that build character.

Quality family time has always been really important to Hannah, so she felt so guilty all of the time. We started to look at her boundaries to see where we could tighten things up and protect what she valued most. We worked to get her out of the prison of overwhelm, exploring ways she could delegate tasks to others, streamline processes and increase efficiency.

The first action we implemented was raising her prices to match the generosity of her giving heart. This increased her profitability to allow her to recruit team members to take things off her plate. I insisted she start using the Eisenhower matrix. She had a habit of prioritising **everything** business-related. Once she learned how to use the matrix, she started moving tasks out of the urgent and important box (top left) and she began to delegate (bottom left).

"Most things which are urgent are not important, and most things which are important are not urgent."

DWIGHT D. EISENHOWER

EISENHOWER MATRIX

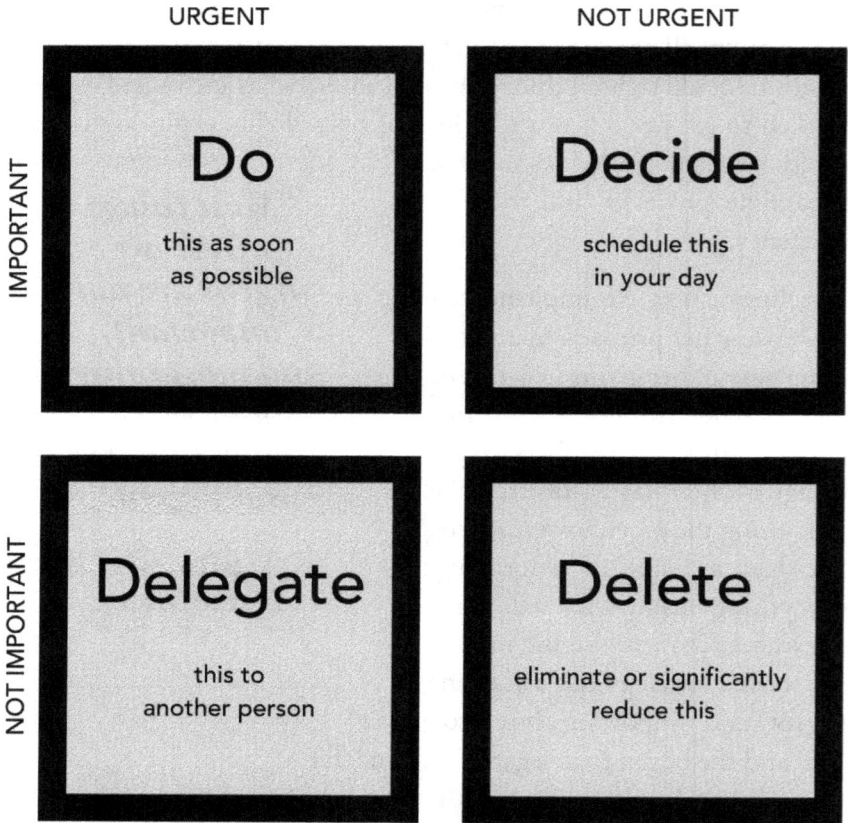

	URGENT	NOT URGENT
IMPORTANT	**Do** this as soon as possible	**Decide** schedule this in your day
NOT IMPORTANT	**Delegate** this to another person	**Delete** eliminate or significantly reduce this

There's a moment in the movie *Jurassic Park* when the character played by Jeff Goldblum says emphatically, "Your scientists were so preoccupied with whether or not they could, they didn't stop to think if they should." Just because Hannah *could* do all the things didn't mean Hannah *should* do all the things. She recruited an incredibly skilled virtual assistant (VA) and learned how to delegate things that she could do, but weren't the best use of her time.

She kept referring to the Eisenhower matrix and together we rewired the subconscious beliefs that were keeping her stuck in what author and Stanford psychologist Gay Hendricks calls the *Zone of Excellence*.

The excellence zone sees us doing things at which we are highly skilled, but it is ultimately unsatisfying because it does not engage our innate individual genius. Being so good at many things meant Hannah was getting constant adrenaline hits from crossing things off her lists. Her subconscious beliefs below saw her regularly working past midnight.

USING THE EISENHOWER MATRIX

It's quite a simple tool that can yield great results when used consistently. To get started, draw the quadrants on a notepad (or digitally if you prefer). Take your to-do list and thoroughly analyse your priorities to determine what goes where then transfer your entire to-do list over. Repeat often.

Do (urgent and important)

- Your most important tasks
- Tasks with a deadline approaching
- Things that cannot be delayed

Example: You send client social media reports at the end of each week and it's Friday morning.

Decide (not urgent and important)

- Regular responsibilities
- Can be scheduled for some other time
- Flexibility in when they are completed

Example: Following up with potential clients needs to happen, but the timing isn't strict. Make sure you allow enough time to execute follow-ups so they don't end up in the 'do' quadrant.

Delegate (urgent and not important)

- Give the impression of being important
- Someone else can do it for you
- Keep you busy and distract you from the 'do' list

Example: Replying to (certain) emails, typing up meeting minutes, sending invoices. If you have a VA, this quadrant is often things they can handle for you.

Delete (not urgent and not important)

- The things you do when you're procrastinating
- Productivity killers
- Don't contribute to your overall goals

Example: Mindless scrolling, checking your phone for calls or messages, procrasti-anything.

JUST BECAUSE YOU CAN...

Just because you can doesn't mean you should. You feel like you are the only one who can do everything you do and that nobody will be as good, as quick or as capable. I hate to break it to you, but you're not so special that you're the *only* person who can create PDFs, edit and upload videos or format your newsletters. This attitude is one of the biggest impediments to business expansion and it's quite common among established businesses. Although Hannah had the resources (budget) to outsource, she kept adding tasks to *her* list. Just because she *could*. A couple of minutes here, a quick task there, yet every little thing she did added up and had snowballed into complete overwhelm.

We're addicted to feeling like we are in control. With this approach, we never give anyone a chance to prove us wrong, and we cling to tasks that completely limit our business growth. So how do we overcome this addiction? The answer lies in a line from one of my favourite songs:

When I first started my business, I helped people with their social media content. I used to think that I had to do everything - the content, graphics *and* scheduling. I sincerely believed that I was the only one who could do it. The client paid *me*, so I thought I had to do *all* the work. It never crossed my mind to enlist some help to free up some time to serve more clients. Then one day I had a lightbulb moment. I couldn't believe how I'd been stifling my business growth. I had a VA creating graphics and scheduling my own content but never thought to delegate client work! Huge aha. I wrote

> *"Let it go, let it goooooooooooo."*
>
> ELSA, FROZEN

up some standard operating procedures (SOPs) and off she went. Tasks instantly went from the upper left quadrant of the Eisenhower matrix (do) to the lower left (delegate).

Mind.

Blown.

Like me, Hannah has learned to let go too. Her new approach is to delegate, asking herself how to get things done without being involved. Her mantra is: *just because I can doesn't mean I should.* She enjoys diversity in her work, but it no longer pushes her to her edge. For Hannah, freedom is a healthy balance between her work and her personal life. Group fitness, relaxing with her family, long walks with her dogs and trying new things. In letting go, she no longer exists inside four walls of a self-imposed prison riddled with overwhelm. She's better at being on time and gets to bed earlier. She has unlocked her version of freedom and enjoys the satisfaction of her efforts.

JOURNAL ACTIVITY: WHERE AM I ROBBING MYSELF?

Grab your journal and spend some time reflecting on the ways you are robbing yourself to give to your business. What overwhelms you the most?

AUDIO PRACTICE: THE MICRO METHOD

We can think of subconscious beliefs as ideas sitting beneath our conscious awareness. They're locked away, informing our reality until we place our attention upon them. One of the practices I used to unlock subconscious beliefs with Hannah is called the Micro Method. It's a simple yet powerful experience that I'd love for you to try no matter how overwhelmed you are, but especially if you identify strongly with the prison of overwhelm. Identify and shift the subconscious belief beneath your overwhelm to unlock your freedom.

Let's make shift happen!

To begin, find yourself a comfortable seat where you won't be disturbed for 20 minutes. Bring to mind something about your business that feels overwhelming, and then press play on this audio I've created for you.

Beating overwhelm may take some time and I invite you to come back and do this exercise every time you start to feel like you have too much on your plate. It's not a one and done. And there are some other keys you can use to take action and free yourself from overwhelm.

WHICH OF THE FOLLOWING KEYS HOLD YOUR FREEDOM?

Here are some more things you can throw at it to break free:

- Cross one thing off your to-do list right now (yes, now)
- Start using the Eisenhower matrix daily
- Admit that you're in way over your head
- Do a brain dump of everything swirling around in your brain
- Start using a regular daily or weekly brain dump
- Get help from someone who can suck out all the stuff in your head and the stuff that's hiding and map it out for you
- Adjust your expectations so that they are realistic
- Create boundaries around time, screens and work hours, and stick to them
- If you aren't already outsourcing, delegate one task
- If you do outsource, get more off your plate by handing over more tasks
- Create SOPs to avoid reinventing the wheel
- Respect and adhere to your work hours
- Create affirmations to rewrite your default behaviour
- Ask another entrepreneur for their input on things you could delegate - be sure to seek a fresh perspective from someone credible
- Book a business audit with me
- Learn to say no, including sometimes saying no to your own ideas

- Honour and protect your personal or social commitments
- Respect and adhere to your bedtime
- Book something that feels indulgent and unnecessary
- Work your discipline muscle
- Set reminders on your phone to alert you when it's time to finish work for the day
- Uncover what being busy means and why you subconsciously value it
- Schedule an energy clearing session with me to clear the addiction to busyness
- Do EFT (tapping) on the frustration you feel about never having enough time
- Work with Ho'oponopono for the guilt you feel about your choices
- Meditate to start your work day
- Incorporate boundaries into your meditation and visualisation practices
- Explore where this shows up in your lineage
- Find ways to acknowledge yourself so that you don't overwork in the pursuit of significance and external validation
- Journal about what overwhelm protects you from
- Visualise how you want your work-life balance to look
- Explore consciousness encoding to move through your blockage
- Do a self-forgiveness practice for 40 days

We now know that the prison of overwhelm impacts your business *and* your personal life. It impacts your choices on the daily. We know that the more capable you are, the more you may feel like you want to 'just get it done.' This prison comes with sacrifices, something always has to give and it's often things or people we love. Action takers are the ones who are most likely to end up in this prison. They just can't help themselves. Just because you can doesn't mean you should! Read through the keys, make a note of the ones you need to implement to free yourself from your prison of overwhelm and put that action-taking to good use.

Chapter 2: Low Self-Esteem
IS LOW SELF-ESTEEM YOUR PRIMARY BUSINESS PRISON?

Your lack of belief in yourself renders you helpless, and your business pays the price. You've turned away from the student within and are subscribing to disempowering stories about yourself. You are more capable than you give yourself credit for. You are selling yourself way too short, but you don't even realise what you are doing.

Consciously or subconsciously, the women in this prison tell themselves stories.

Here are some examples of how this prison shows up:

- Technology is too hard; you believe you're no good with computers
- You have no idea what you're doing
- You often think, *'Maybe I'm not cut out for this'*
- You're too spiritual to have structure
- You over-deliver to make it feel like you've given value (e.g. your sessions frequently go over time to make up for feeling like what you do isn't enough)
- You don't *really* want the success that you say you want because you believe that you can't do it (read: you don't want to put in the effort to achieve it)
- If you don't give 100%, then you won't feel like a total failure when you don't achieve something, because you can pretend (or hide behind) not really caring or trying
- You don't want to implement procedures and stifle your flow; you prefer to work intuitively

- You can't plan your quarter let alone your year; it's too hard to think so long-term

- You prefer your comfort zone

- You talk about and avoid discomfort but you never actually move through it

Negative subconscious beliefs associated with this prison

- I don't know what I'm doing

- I'm not good enough

- I don't deserve abundance or success

- I'm a fraud

- I am unworthy of success

- I can either be in flow or organised, but not both

- I am insignificant

- If they find out I don't have it all together, I'll look like an imposter

- I can't trust others

- I'm making it all up

- Success is for others, not for me

As you can see, this entrepreneurial prison shows up in many ways. Let's explore an example from my client Elle, an incredible woman who was stuck in a prison of her own making.

Prisoner story: Elle the Energy Worker

In one of our Zoom sessions, I caught Elle saying that she wasn't good with technology, systems, or her business's 'back end'. Instead of stoking the fire of her business with possibilities, she was pouring her potential down the drain with the words she spoke.

> *"Nourish and encourage the entrepreneur in you, or you'll revert back to, 'I don't know how to get there,' and stop thinking big."*
>
> MARGARET M LYNCH

One of my specialties is shining a light on patterns and behaviours in the blind spot of entrepreneurs, so I brought it to her attention, illuminating how she was subtly discrediting herself. She was blown away. She had no idea how frequently she was doing it. I illustrated how she was perpetuating this limiting belief about herself and encoding her reality with more of the same bullshit story. She was bumping up against one of the immutable hermetic cosmic laws, the Law of Correspondence: as within, so without. As Ricci-Jane Adams explains in her book *Spiritually Fierce*, our inner thoughts and feelings manifest their exact likeness in our external reality. Technology and systems felt complicated and overwhelming; Elle lacked organisation behind the scenes and wasn't treating her business seriously.

Imposter Syndrome

> *"Some tasks build competence, and some build character."*
>
> JAY SHETTY

Imposter Syndrome is a term that was coined in 1978 by two clinical psychologists, Dr Pauline Clance and Dr Suzanne Imes. It describes the all-too-common experience whereby we believe we don't really know what we're doing, are not qualified enough, chalking our success up to luck. Imposter Syndrome is a key indicator that you are in the low self-esteem prison.

As the founder of HelloSeven Rachel Rodgers explains in her book *We Should All Be Millionaires*, many of us get stuck in the trap of Imposter Syndrome. She hits the nail on the head with this: "You work for free, or undercharge for your work because you're terrified that you suck." Rodgers goes on to suggest that Imposter Syndrome is keeping you broke. One study showed that Imposter Syndrome is the reason 55% of self-employed women automatically discount their prices before a client even asks for a lower price. WTAF?! Fifty-five percent is huge! Based on this, there's a pretty good chance that you don't give yourself *nearly* enough credit. You hold yourself back because deep down you believe that you're just not good enough. So pause for a moment, close your eyes and give yourself a little fist-bump for something you did well. Yes, I want you to do it now. I'll wait.

Now, let's get back to Elle. Realising that she frequently discredited herself, albeit subconsciously, Elle decided to create a different reality for herself and her business. So we set out to change the narrative, to consciously curate her story using curiosity, innocence and open-heartedness. We cleared the subconscious belief and then Elle got to work reframing her stories. I was delighted to receive a voice message from Elle, informing me that she had completed her homework. A diligent client, she dismantled her stale helplessness language and created new power statements.

Here's what she came up with:

- I am ready, willing and able to learn
- I am looking forward to creating clear structures and systems so that the back end of my business flows with ease
- I can achieve all that I set my mind to
- I am learning new things, and it is fun

- I enjoy exploring the layers of this structured business framework, and I love the payoff from this

Elle reframed her helplessness language and claimed the key to her freedom. If she ever catches herself using the old story, she replaces it with something from her new narrative.

Goodbye prison, hello free empowered woman!

JOURNAL ACTIVITY: HELPLESS TO HELPFUL

Grab your journal and spend some time reflecting on Elle's story. In your journal, answer these two questions: What unhelpful or disempowering stories am I telling myself about my capabilities? In what ways am I identifying with or perpetuating my own helplessness?

German Philosopher Nietzsche said that one of the best days in his life was the day when he rebaptised all his negative qualities as his best qualities. If you've been telling yourself helplessness stories, they've probably been on repeat for a while, lifetimes perhaps. The first step in rewriting the story is identifying the dominant narrative. Next, give yourself 20 minutes of undisturbed and uninterrupted time with your journal.

AUDIO PRACTICE: WHAT'S YOUR STORY?

Close your eyes as you listen to this short audio, and allow yourself to feel and experience each sentence. Once you've listened to it once, pop it on again and when you find a sentence you like, make a note of it in your journal. If it sparks ideas for other powerful statements, write those down too.

Add positive versions of the disempowering stories you've been telling yourself and the ways you've been robbing yourself to give to your business. Write until you fill at least one page. These are your new stories, and it's time for you to claim them. You may like to put your favourite on your phone, your computer screensaver, or a sticky note on the fridge. Some of my clients even write them in lipstick on the bathroom mirror. Then look at the keys below to see which ones speak to you. Make a note of the ones that resonate, and get to work. These keys will help you reclaim your power and kick helplessness to the curb.

You can further enhance this practice by starting with the Micro Method practice from Chapter 1.

WHICH OF THE FOLLOWING KEYS HOLD YOUR FREEDOM?

- Pay close attention to the words you say
- Reframe your language, e.g. 'I'm not good with X' becomes 'I am learning how to do better with X'
- Get humble enough to adopt a student mindset
- Claim your expertise
- Stop comparing yourself to others
- Remember that you can be spiritual *and* have great systems
- Make an effort to be a graceful learner
- Book a session with me and plan to hand over tasks that feel hard
- Hire a VA
- Recognise your optimal work hours and adjust your schedule accordingly
- Notice where you drastically underestimate how long something takes
- Read *The Big Leap* by Gay Hendricks

- Get help with the things that are outside your Zone of Genius
- Connect with other women who are also running businesses
- Create affirmations to build your confidence
- Get out of your office and work from somewhere different and fresh
- Get a mentor or coach
- Don't be so stubborn that you don't ever ask for help
- Find a coworking buddy
- If you're a millennial, read *Earth is Hiring* by Peta Kelly
- Purchase a hypnosis track to boost your self-esteem
- Attend networking and connecting events
- Out yourself by sending me a message on Facebook or Instagram
- Take back your power from all the places you've left it
- Let go of perfectionism
- Give up your martyrdom
- Book an energy clearing session with me to clear the addiction to your faulty belief about yourself
- Uncover the root cause of your self-doubt
- Apply the Micro Method liberally
- Journal on the impact of your low self-esteem
- Use EFT to clear the belief from your subtle anatomy
- Visualise your solar plexus chakra (the energy centre above your navel) cleansed and free from blockages
- Incorporate positive statements in your meditation practice

Is Your Business a Prison?

As you read through the keys, make a note of the ones you need to implement to free yourself from your prison of low self-esteem. Make a commitment to change the negative inner dialogue that is imprisoning you. When you recognise the impact your words have on creating your reality, you begin to take back your power. Even the best business ideas can be thwarted by low self-esteem because the stories in your conscious reasoning and your subconscious mind determine your business trajectory, and only you can rewrite the narrative. This prison is a great example of the power of our words, so what story will you tell?

Chapter 3: All The Things
IS DOING 'ALL THE THINGS' YOUR PRIMARY BUSINESS PRISON?

Your inability to pick one thing and stick to it for more than five minutes is suffocating your business. Before you give one idea a chance to succeed, you move on to the next idea and in doing so, you crush its potential to flourish. You rarely follow through on a project, service or offer because you chop and change so often. You are proud to be multi-passionate and believe strongly that curiosity and learning are essential for continued personal growth. You are not known for *one* thing because you pursue all of your passions, and immediately convert what you learn into something to sell. When people ask you what you do, you rattle off a list of qualifications. The list is so long that you need to stop to take a breath halfway, just to get through them all.

Here are some examples of how this prison shows up:

- You are multi-passionate and proud of it
- You want to share everything you've learned with others
- You choose what feels comfortable over what is strategic and most profitable
- You feel like you're always in startup
- Ideas flow to you, and you grab each one and run with it
- You're a naturally curious lifelong learner
- You can help people in so many ways
- It's hard to introduce yourself because you have so much to say

- You resist having a niche or an ideal client because you can help anyone

- Your flow of clients is inconsistent

- When ideas and inspiration land, you share them immediately

- Your loyal clients support everything you do, but you feel like you're still just starting out over and over

- You can't seem to create lasting success

Negative subconscious beliefs associated with this prison

- I'll never be good enough

- I need more qualifications

- I don't know what I'm doing

- I don't deserve abundance

- I am unworthy of effortless success

- I don't trust myself

- It's never enough; I always need more

You download new ideas and put them straight onto social media. You don't bother to map things out, or use any strategy. You neglect the customer experience because you are so excited that you don't even consider it. Your business lacks maturity.

"The essence of strategy is choosing what not to do."

PROF. MICHAEL PORTER

Prisoner story: Stacey the Spiritual Healer

When I met her, I could tell straight away that Stacey was good at many things and an absolute powerhouse – intuitive, passionate, motivated and inspiring. While Stacey was intelligent, she was also addicted to learning new things so she easily got distracted by 'bright shiny objects.' She was always enrolled in some new course, doing more study, participating in an online challenge, attending an event or a retreat. There is nothing wrong with learning and personal development (quite the opposite, in fact), but Stacey was always in a *pursuing* energy, never pausing long enough to anchor the knowledge into something enduring. As soon as she would complete a course, she added it to her list of services, and as you can imagine, the list was loooooong. Herein lay the problem. Even though Stacey had been self-employed for some time, her business never felt like it got beyond startup.

She found it difficult to explain what she did when she attended networking events. She could easily list all of her qualifications and modalities, but what was missing for Stacey was knowing how to articulate the **outcome** that she helped her clients to achieve. Stacey struggled because she kept chopping and changing what she offered instead of leading with the transformation she would facilitate. Clients don't care about modalities; they care about how you make them **feel**.

> *"Ideas are abundant among entrepreneurs, but it doesn't mean you follow through with all of them."*
>
> KRIS EMERY, EDITOR

In Stacey's world, it's hard to gain momentum, income is sporadic, and everything feels chaotic. Others can't confidently recommend Stacey because they don't trust that she'll be selling the same thing next month. Word of mouth has the power to drum up loads of new business, yet Stacey was unpredictable and shooting herself in the foot.

Instead of choosing *one* thing to focus on, Stacey was spread too thin and nobody *really* knew or understood what she did. Stacey needed to lead with something. The more specific, the better. Yet like so many entrepreneurs I come across, she was resisting being specific. Stacey has studied reiki, sound healing, Access Bars and Hawaiian massage, so here are some examples of how she can be more specific.

- I use reiki to help high-achieving women in corporate relieve the stress of their jobs
- I'm a sound healer for socially anxious women in their twenties who find it challenging to be in big crowds
- I'm a hands-on Access Bars practitioner, and I reduce the severity and frequency of headaches for exhausted mothers of neurodiverse children
- I offer kahuna massage for hospital workers who feel disconnected from their emotions because of the tragedies they witness

JOURNAL ACTIVITY: YOUR TURN

Now it's your turn. Firstly, notice how specific the examples are. Can you think of some examples in your own community? Try writing a couple down before writing your own.

If you get stuck

The examples listed all describe Stacey, and if she just chose one, people would easily identify that she was the right person for them. Let me explain. Imagine I twist and hurt my ankle while bushwalking with my friend Deb. Deb knows I'm into holistic healing, and I live an active lifestyle, including volleyball and yoga. She is the kind of friend who tags me on Facebook for things she thinks I will like. Imagine Deb is scrolling Facebook the next day, and sees a Facebook ad for a physiotherapist. She scrolls past, and 5 minutes later she sees another ad for a physiotherapist, but this one specialises in ankles and treats active people with a holistic approach. Which Facebook ad do you think my friend Deb will tag me in?

I've put together a few more examples to help you write yours. Remember, specificity is essential!

- I'm a period coach for tweens, helping them navigate the changes to their bodies so they become confident to manage their periods when with their peers

- I'm a photographer for self-employed women who are self-conscious about their weight but want to update their branding photos

- I'm a health coach who helps women with fibromyalgia reduce and manage their symptoms through food

- I'm a post-mastectomy boudoir photographer who helps women feel beautiful after their surgery

- I help new mums to achieve their breastfeeding goals even though their GP has told them to give up

- I source fresh organic produce from local farmers and deliver it to busy health-conscious families in Brisbane

- I teach artists how to make money from their art by using Etsy

- I offer pregnancy yoga for first-time mothers who have trouble sleeping

- I run a wholefoods cafe that sources and sells local products

- I run gentle fitness classes for retirees with arthritis and osteoporosis

- I run a clinic for women in menopause who feel like they've tried everything to relieve their symptoms

Is Your Business a Prison?

Once you've written yours, make sure you send them to me. Find my business on socials and drop me a message to share your work. Be sure to tell me that you're reading my book, and I'll offer you some feedback on what you've written!

If you're not yet convinced…

I've been there. In 2015, I won an all-expenses-paid trip to Bali. The competition was a lip-sync battle created by business mentor Tash Corbin. Fun right? To watch my video submission, head to the resources page for this book (www.chenaecarey.com/bookresources). The prize was a personalised business mentoring retreat with Tash, who was living in Bali at the time. I will never forget when she asked about my business and what I did. I wanted to be a one-stop marketing shop and I showed her the services page on my website:

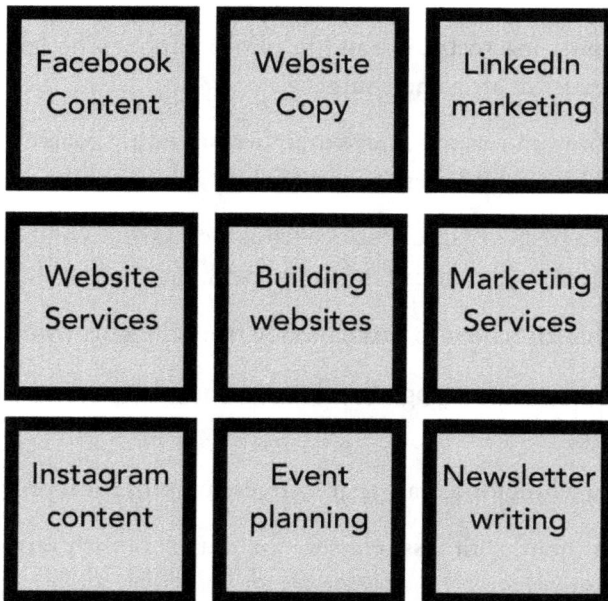

Facebook Content	Website Copy	LinkedIn marketing
Website Services	Building websites	Marketing Services
Instagram content	Event planning	Newsletter writing

She gently suggested that I'd need to pick *one* thing from the list and my thoughts went a little something like this:

One thing? Just one? But I can do all of these things! Why would I just pick one? Is she serious? Why wouldn't I offer all the things I can do? I don't want to exclude potential customers. Why would I turn down work? This is madness! I need to get clients, not turn them away. I've put so much work into creating this. I can't possibly ditch the majority of it! This can't be right.

I didn't say any of these things aloud, but I can assure you I thought them all, and then some! I couldn't believe what she was suggesting. Luckily for me, I trusted Tash enough to grit my teeth and choose one. I put all my eggs into one basket and came back from that retreat intent on claiming my one thing. I trusted her advice and chose Facebook marketing. I chose *one thing*, and it worked.

The decision changed the trajectory of my business. It served me well when my day job was made redundant. It set me up for success. I didn't think I could be specific, but I did it. If I can, you can.

Many of my clients have been through a similar experience with me. I've asked them to make their work narrow and specific, and they resisted. They resisted a *lot*. I witnessed their resistance, and if I'm honest, I was not particularly popular going through this process with them, but I didn't mind. There is so much untapped potential on the other side of this process. Choosing *one* thing is crucial to a solid business foundation, and I am living proof that *it works*. Was it comfortable? Not at all. Yet my willingness to make that decision has paid off many times.

> *"Once you become known for one thing,*
> *it's easy to become known for a second thing, a third thing, and a fourth thing."*
>
> ROBERT SCOBLE

Pivots in business are pretty common. I've done two significant pivots myself. Knowing the importance of choosing *one* thing has served me incredibly well during those pivots. Much of my audience came with me when I first pivoted because I'd developed trust. They could rely upon me to stick to one thing. As my direction shifted, most of them remained on my mailing list and in my social media audience.

AUDIO PRACTICE: HEART CONGRUENCE

The idea of picking and sticking to one thing can stir up some fear. *What about everything else I can do? Won't I be excluding some of the people I can help? I don't want anyone to miss out.*

The result is usually discomfort in the form of stress, worry, doubt and anxiety, especially if this is your dominant prison. Heart Congruence is the antidote. It's one of my favourite ways to raise my vibration - a simple practice adapted from the HeartMath Institute's Heart Coherence practice. We withdraw our energy and attention from the external world and focus on cultivating a high vibrational feeling state such as gratitude, joy, abundance, freedom. Since your vibration informs your reality and your vibration is relative to your feeling state, find yourself a moment when you won't be disturbed, and listen to this audio.

WHICH OF THE FOLLOWING KEYS HOLD YOUR FREEDOM?

- Pick one thing and stick to it for one, three, or even six months
- Send me a message to share your one thing
- Put reminders on your phone that say 'I am qualified enough'
- Pursue other training for personal use only for the next twelve months
- Stop adding every qualification you have to your services list
- Create a self-imposed ban on buying new courses, enrolling in new programs
- Consolidate everything you do into *one* key offering

- Stop pivoting every five minutes

- Create consistent sales of *one* thing before you begin to market another

- If you feel particularly stressed, you can extend Heart Congruence into the Micro Method

- Get comfortable with saying the same thing; you are *meant* to be on repeat

- Create affirmations to cultivate more stability

- Out yourself by sending me a message on Facebook or Instagram, telling me your prison

- Do a 'letting go' meditation

- Read *The Genius Zone* by Gay Hendricks

- Uncover why you feel like you're never enough by exploring your dominant subconscious story

- Find out which lifetime you took on the belief that you're not enough just as you are

- Release the need to study more

- Uncover what picking one thing means and why you subconsciously avoid it

- Journal on what being specific means to you and why you're afraid of it

- Use EFT to clear your niche resistance

- Visualise your ideal client, and what their day looks like

- During your meditation practice, cultivate the feelings you want your ideal client to feel

Is Your Business a Prison?

We know that trying to serve everyone doesn't do your business any favours, and that specificity is key. You now understand the importance of being able to clearly articulate the outcomes you help your clients achieve. While your modalities make you the incredible practitioner you are today, communicating the *outcomes* is crucial. If you see yourself in Stacey and you'd like to become clear and articulate about your work, it's entirely possible! It's also okay if you need help. Get started with the keys by committing to taking action on the ones you need to implement to free yourself from this prison.

Chapter 4: Who To Trust
IS KNOWING WHO TO TRUST YOUR PRIMARY BUSINESS PRISON?

You don't trust yourself because you are scared. You are scared of doing something you've never done. What if you fail? You are nervous about saying something that will rock the boat. What if your friends or family disagree? You are afraid to back yourself. What if you stopped trying to fit in and it backfired? You don't want to make an impact and end up standing out for the wrong reasons. You are terrified of discomfort, so you ignore those inklings. You'd rather someone tell you what to do, because if it doesn't work out, it's *their* fault. You are outsourcing your sovereignty because you've forgotten how to trust yourself. Your business pays the price for this total lack of trust in your intuition. You doubt your ability to make the right decision for your business. You don't behave like the CEO.

Here are some examples of how this prison shows up:

- You want someone to tell you what to do
- You get a feeling, a sense of what you should do, but it's scary so you dismiss it
- You rely heavily upon coaches and mentors
- You want to buy all the courses that promise to solve your problems and challenges
- You're more likely to bury your head in the sand than risk discomfort or failure
- People are often waiting for you to make up your mind

- You feel like you are listening to so many different voices and expert opinions that you're totally confused

- When it gets too hard, you avoid making decisions

- You love it when someone tells you exactly what to do so you don't have to carry the burden of making the right decision

- You get stuck if you have to make a difficult decision

- You listen to the cacophony of voices in the marketing world and use your confusion as an excuse for your inaction

- Giving 'guru' status to coaches and mentors is normal for you

- You sometimes regret not trusting your intuition, and in hindsight, you say things like 'I should have known' and 'I knew better'

Negative subconscious beliefs associated with this prison

- I don't trust myself

- I'm not good enough

- I don't trust my intuition

- My head rules my world

- I am terrified of failure

- I can't trust others

- I'm afraid of authority

Trusting yourself is trusting your intuition. Before you make any assumptions about whether you're intuitive or not, I want you to know that intuition is not a special gift bestowed upon a select few. It's innate, biological. If you have a pulse, which I know you do, you are intuitive. You can think of your intuition as listening to your heart. You may ignore the whispers of your heart *thinking* you know better. I bet you even have days where you don't trust yourself because you believe that someone else knows better.

Prisoner story: Anna the Acupuncturist

When Anna came to me, she was frustrated. Most of her clients were making her life hard. They rescheduled at the last minute, paid their invoices late and were often late to sessions but still expected the entire hour. They refused to use Anna's booking system and expected her to do all the work. It wasn't unusual for her partner and friends to hear Anna complain about her clients. She had the occasional client who was punctual, reliable and paid their invoices on time, but the rest were so difficult that she sometimes doubted whether her business was worth it.

Here's what I saw. Anna's clients were not the problem. The common denominator was Anna. She kept working with clients who weren't a good fit because of fear. She was scared to say no. I knew Anna, and I knew she could intuitively spot a troublesome client a mile away, but she didn't want to miss out on the income. She abandoned her innate knowing and operated from fear. This meant Anna was working twice as hard, investing more time and energy than she should. The stress hormones associated with fear are addictive. People like Anna burn out.

JOURNAL ACTIVITY: HEAD OR HEART?

Grab a pen and make a list of ten decisions you've made in your business. Mix them up, including big decisions and less significant ones. Here are some examples to get you started:

- Going over time with a client session
- Creating a new product or service
- Pivoting your offering

- Asking for a testimonial
- Investing in a customer relationship management (CRM)
- Saying yes to a podcast interview
- Hiring a VA
- Writing one of last week's Instagram posts
- Choosing a platform (e.g. Xero, Mailchimp, Zoom, Acuity)
- Increasing your prices
- Discontinuing a membership
- Doing your own bookkeeping
- Running a low-cost workshop
- Paying for a program upfront
- Upgrading to Canva Pro
- Offering a discount
- Attending a networking event
- Saying yes to that new client
- Signing up for a course
- Delegating tasks
- Getting professional branding

Now reflect on each decision. Which decisions were made with your head? What about your heart? How many times did your logic and intuition work together? Pause for a moment and deeply consider what this list means and what it says about your business decision-making process. I believe that we need both - inspiration and strategy. How balanced are your decisions?

INTUITION AND DISCOMFORT

It's exciting when your intuition guides you to create a new program, product or service. It's pretty easy to trust those nudges, right? But what happens when your intuition suggests you discontinue something? Or say no to a potential client? That's scary, and there's no guarantee that you'll ever uncover *why*.

Fear is what hands our decision-making over to our conscious reasoning mind. Anna's heart knew that saying no to that potential client was the right thing to do, but her head was afraid to lose the sale. Many of us privilege our heads over our hearts because we prefer to feel like we are in control. Our constant need for control is why I do *intuitive* business mentoring. I guide my clients intuitively, beyond their logic and reason. I act as a conduit for the infinite intelligence trying to reach them.

When your head overrides your heart, you're operating from fear. If your heart overrides your head, you're neglecting an essential element of business success – strategy. Anna's conscious reasoning mind and her divine intuitive self must work together. When they do, Anna has all the answers. She might not like the answers, but she knows, feels, sees or senses them. Aligned clients flow to Anna when she trusts herself. Decision-making doesn't feel like running in concrete boots. Her choices feel good.

When I look at my own journey, I can't deny the inherent interconnectedness between business growth and trusting my intuition. More trust resulted in more expansion. I trusted myself to explore Insight Timer in 2020 and in 2021 I was headhunted by their publishing team for their @Work mindfulness program. The first course I published on Insight Timer generated almost $1,000 AUD in leveraged income in the first month.

When my head and heart work together, I make strong decisions. Do the same, and you'll free yourself from the burden of fear, your intuition will become your invisible business partner, and deep wisdom will guide you. Intuition is innate; we all have it. But it's like a muscle; it gets stronger the more you work it. If you have no idea how to access your intuition, or you'd like to get to know it more intimately, the next practice is for you.

WHAT IS YOUR DOMINANT CLAIR?

I learned from Dr Ricci-Jane Adams that we all have a dominant intuitive skill. Uncovering and learning about my dominant clair (clairsentience) was really helpful when I first started learning about my intuition because I was soooooo in my head. Intuition is subtle, so it gave me - a classic overthinker - something to look out for. It helped me work out what was my intuition and what might just be coming from my conscious reasoning mind.

Everyone has each of these four clairs (and others), and we all have a dominant clair. Your dominant intuitive skill will be one of the following four clairs.

Clairsentience – clear feeling

Clairaudience – clear hearing

Clairvoyance – clear seeing

Clairsentience – clear knowing

These clairs are non-local versions of your dominant senses. To give you an example of what this means, clairvoyance doesn't mean you are seeing with your eyes; it's *symbolic* sight. You will see images and visuals with your mind's eye. Clairaudience doesn't mean hearing with your ears, but you might hear words whispered to you, you might notice sounds, songs or information being 'spoken' in your mind.

It might be tempting to try to guess what your dominant clair might be, but I encourage you to come into the practice below without any preconceived notions. Trust me when I say it makes the experience a little easier if you let go of everything you *think* you know!

AUDIO PRACTICE: IDENTIFY YOUR DOMINANT CLAIR

This audio practice is designed to help you uncover your dominant clair. You'll be guided into a meditative state, and then invited to ask yourself a question. When the time comes to ask the question, try not to focus so much on the answer itself, but *how* you receive the answer. Do you know it? Feel it? Hear it? See it? Pay close attention to what comes first. If your mind is busy, get out of your head and into your heart with the Heart Congruence practice first.

> *"Intuition is a spiritual faculty and does not explain, but simply points the way."*
>
> FLORENCE SCOVEL SHINN

WHICH OF THE FOLLOWING KEYS HOLD YOUR FREEDOM?

- Own your decisions
- Stop worrying so much about what other people think
- Work with affirmations and start to create a new reality
- Give up your addiction to victimhood
- Read *Think Like a Monk* by Jay Shetty
- Change your phone screensaver to something that reminds you to trust your intuition
- Learn how to trust and act upon your intuition
- Stop making choices from fear

Is Your Business a Prison?

- Allow your heart and head to work as a team

- Read *The Surrender Experiment* by Michael J Singer

- Write reminders on your mirror, fridge or the back of your toilet door

- Pay attention to your business decisions and reflect on how they were made

- Stop outsourcing your sovereignty

- Ignore cheap silver-bullet input and instead privilege rich, detailed, thorough and substantial wisdom

- Own your shadow by sending me a message on Facebook or Instagram to share the ways in which this prison shows up for you

- Claim the role of CEO and act the part

- Start your day with meditation to listen to your heart

- Release your need to control everything (e.g. work with a practitioner)

- Do the Micro Method daily for at least seven days

- Pause each day to take a few deep breaths and shift out of your busy beta brainwave state

- Uncover why you don't trust yourself

- Commit to learning more about your intuition

- Explore where you might be the common denominator and adjust accordingly

- When you have a crisis of confidence, try tapping

- Journal on your beliefs about trust

- Use EFT to clear your distrust in your intuitive knowing

- Visualise yourself claiming your intuition and weaving it into your business decisions

- Explore aligning with your highest self in your meditation practice

We now understand that your head and heart make a powerful team. As a heart-centred business person, you can harness an extraordinary amount of wisdom and guidance if you tap into your intuition. When you trust yourself and claim your sovereignty, you position yourself as an expert. It's undeniable. I want that for you. I hope you do too.

If you see yourself in Anna's story, perhaps you're ready to free yourself from this prison. To learn how to connect to your intuition and trust it, I've got a short course on Insight Timer to help with that. It's called Intuition for Small Businesses.

Chapter 5: Comfort Zone

IS STAYING IN YOUR COMFORT ZONE YOUR PRIMARY BUSINESS PRISON?

Your lifestyle is smack bang in the middle of your comfort zone. Sometimes things are good, sometimes it's not so great, but it's manageable. You just ride the waves. Things have been this way for so long that they have become normal. You feel unfulfilled. Your daily life lacks vigour, you often feel devoid of passion and excitement, and most days are deeply unsatisfying. You are settling because you are terrified to make changes. It impacts your relationships, your lifestyle, your business.

Here are some examples of how this prison shows up:

- You've experienced success but can't seem to get back there
- Clients flow in and then dry up
- Feeling stuck and unable to shift out of it is normal for you
- You are living a comfortable life that doesn't delight you
- You've experienced business growth but it's limited
- You are banging your head against a brick wall
- You feel comfortable to take small risks for small rewards, nothing too drastic
- You stay in relationships that aren't working
- You feel deeply unfulfilled but you are unwilling to make risky changes
- If you are truly honest with yourself, you are settling

Negative subconscious beliefs associated with this prison

- If I succeed, I'll lose everything
- I am afraid of being alone
- I'll always have to sacrifice
- I don't deserve to have it all
- Things never go well for me
- Something always has to give
- I don't trust myself
- I am insignificant
- I can't trust others
- Success isn't safe for me

You're stuck in a funk because significant business success means that life as you know it will change forever. Wildly abundant success means giving up your comfort zone, but you're wedded to it, hanging on with white knuckles. Ever heard anyone say they're stuck in a funk? Perhaps you've said it yourself. When you're in a funk, you don't know if anything you have built will survive if you risk pursuing success, so succeeding terrifies you. You unconsciously sabotage your business success in an effort to remain in your comfort zone.

> *"Life is either a daring adventure, or nothing at all."*
>
> HELEN KELLER

Caroline Myss would describe this behaviour as the shadow archetype of the prostitute. Now, before you get any ideas, this archetype is not about sex in exchange for money, but it does involve an exchange of sorts. When you are in the shadow archetype of the prostitute, you negotiate your power for security. You sell out your desire for passion,

56

purpose, vitality and joy and settle for the mundane inside your comfort zone.

Prisoner story: Alana the Abundance & Mindset Practitioner

When I first met Alana, she was working in an unfulfilling job. While she was good at the job, she was miserable. Alana felt stuck. Not only did she need the money, but her work was in the family business. She wholeheartedly believed that it would be disastrous if she left. What if they never spoke to her again, completely disowning her? Wasn't she obliged to stick it out because that's what family does? Wouldn't leaving be letting everybody down? She was terrified because she could only imagine the worst-case scenario.

Alana had a business on the side that she was desperate to get up and running. She yearned deeply for a business that lit her up *and* met her family's financial needs. Instead of chasing that dream, she was stagnant, unhappy and unsatisfied. Leaving the family business never seemed like an option. To free herself from the funk she was stuck in, she needed to break her addiction to the comfort zone that imprisoned her.

> *"The comfort zone is nothing else but a graveyard for your dreams and ideas."*
>
> ANONYMOUS

Through our work together, I supported Alana to see beyond the worst-case scenario. I helped her summon the courage to resign. Feeling empowered, she left the family business and broke her addiction to her comfort zone. I introduced her to someone in my network who would be interested in employing someone with her skills, and the rest is history. Her new position allowed her to continue contributing to the household income *and* pursue her own business. If you ask her, Alana will tell you it wasn't easy. It was scary and uncomfortable, but she'd make that same decision every time if she had to do it all again. She now has a business she loves, making a difference in a way that lights her up like a Christmas tree on Christmas Eve. Her willingness to give up her comfort zone saw her entire world change. Alana is free.

Many people spend their entire lives in their comfort zone, plodding along, feeling '*meh*' at best. I don't know about you, but that is *not* how I want to live my life. My business coach and money mentor Laura Elkaslassy once asked me a potent question that I want to share with you. Please consider this question deeply:

Is your business by design or by default?

During 2020, I became sedentary, using the pandemic as an excuse to be lazy, eat shit food, do the bare minimum in my business. I put on weight.

> *"When we spend our lives waiting until we're perfect or bulletproof before we walk into the arena, we ultimately sacrifice opportunities, squander our precious time and turn our backs on precious gifts that are the unique contribution that only we can make."*
>
> BRENÉ BROWN

I had very little energy. I'd become wedded to my comfort zone and lost my zest for life. After doing the practice below, I realised that I was doing business (and life) by default. I immediately got to work.

Within months, I became the strongest, fittest, healthiest, happiest, wealthiest and the most fulfilled I've ever been. Living a life by design gives me an incredible sense of freedom. I do beach yoga most days, walk to the supermarket, play beach volleyball every week, outsource my meal prep to local businesses (run by women, of course), and take belly-dancing classes. This freedom flows into my business and the wheels keep spinning.

AUDIO PRACTICE: TURN YOUR FOCUS WITHIN

This is a reflective audio practice designed to prepare you for the activity below. Don't read ahead. Just find yourself a comfortable seat where you won't be disturbed. Ideally, you have time available to complete the practice below immediately after completing this audio practice.

JOURNAL ACTIVITY: WHEEL OF LIFE

Grab your journal and follow the steps below.

Step 1: Draw a large circle, filling the page.

Step 2: Create eight segments to make a wheel.

Step 3: Label each segment, using wheel #1 below (life).

Step 4: On a new page, give each segment some context, what it means to you. For example, health might include food, energy levels, sport, strength and exercise. Or it might mean weight, blood pressure, sleep and nutrition. Create your own definition.

Step 5: Give yourself a score out of ten for each element.

Step 6: Repeat the same process for wheel #2 (business).

Wheel 1: Life	Wheel 2: Business
▪ Health	▪ Foundations
▪ Relationships	▪ Energy
▪ Surroundings/environment	▪ Systems
▪ Money	▪ Clients
▪ Career	▪ Money
▪ Personal growth	▪ Quality
▪ Vitality/joy	▪ Marketing
▪ Spiritual life	▪ Mentoring

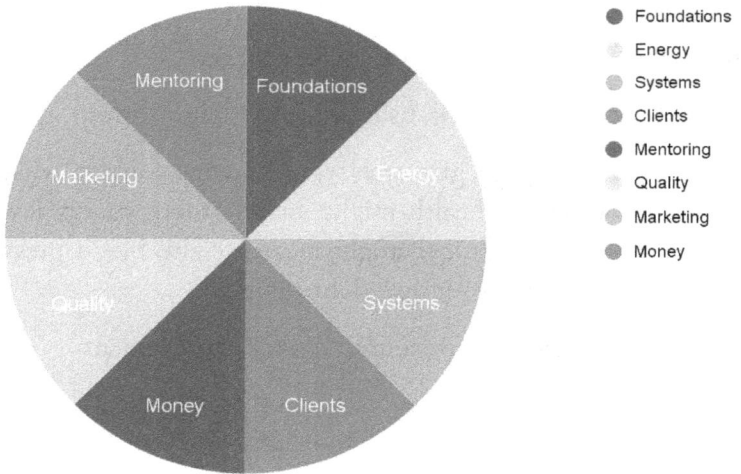

BONUS ACTIVITY: GO DEEPER

Once complete, reflect on your scores. What needs to change? Set goals and intentions to help you create the changes you want to see using the examples below and the word list to inspire you.

Brightness of life

- I will create unique experiences with my friends and loved ones that captivate and fascinate

- I will sign up for the (painting/dancing/Spanish) classes I keep putting off

Money

- I will create more financial abundance and spaciousness by selling the things I no longer need

"Spend time each week purposely sitting in the entrepreneurial mindset of picturing and dreaming. Whether you take an hour or even 10 minutes, that's more visionary thinking than 90% of small business owners and solopreneurs do in six months."

Margaret M Lynch

- I will read *Tapping Into Wealth* by Margaret M Lynch to set money goals, clear my baggage and create more wealth

Is Your Business a Prison?

Surroundings/environment

- I choose to liberate myself by decluttering unwanted gifts, clothes, kitchen cupboards or the garage, only keeping things that bring me pleasure

- I will purchase new bedding that feels luxurious, with zero guilt about the cost

Marketing

- I choose to set aside time every month to dress up and record some video content for my list, allowing my newsletter audience to see my passion

- I will curate stimulating conversation starters for my social media audience

Mentoring

- I commit to working with a business mentor to keep me motivated

- I limit the input that I receive to those I trust and align with

Business foundations

- I commit to creating solid business foundations

- I prioritise organising what I need

Word list for goal-setting

- Blissful
- Joyful
- Abundant
- Delightful
- Pleasurable
- Captivating
- Humbling
- Thrilling
- Happy
- Soft
- Liberating
- Passionate
- Fascinating
- Soulful
- Gratifying
- Enjoyable
- Wild
- Ecstatic
- Luxurious
- Peaceful
- Dazzling
- Profitable
- Rewarding
- Enchanting
- Spacious
- Organised
- Hysterical
- Stimulating
- Enthralling
- Momentous

WHICH OF THE FOLLOWING KEYS HOLD YOUR FREEDOM?

- Take ownership of your comfort zone by sending me a message on Facebook or Instagram and telling me how you've been holding yourself back

- Pursue the lowest areas in your wheels with passion and focus

- Write down all the ways your comfort zone is suffocating your business growth

- Set a new goal each time you achieve one from your list

- Have an honest conversation with a trusted confidant about where you think you've sold out your passion in exchange for security

- Sell something you've kept out of obligation

- Use this journal prompt: *is my business by design or by default?*

- Set reminders of your intentions on your phone

- Get support with your visibility and do something bold

- Share your goals with others and keep each other accountable

- Explore unique ways to improve your scores

- Read *Dying to be Me* by Anita Moorjani

- Uncover the importance of the comfort zone and why you subconsciously value it

- Apply the Micro Method liberally and regularly

- Work with a practitioner to support your nervous system to feel safe as you make changes

- Create affirmations that tell a different story

- Journal on what would bring more brightness into your business

- Use EFT to release the fear of trying new things, taking risks and getting things wrong

- Visualise yourself taking a leap of faith and everything working out

- Explore Insight Timer for meditations on courage

- Write down everything that scares you

- Create a unique experience that brings brightness into your life

- Look for what you aspire to among your peers

- Commit to doing one thing each day that stretches your comfort zone

- Use your meditation practice to calm your body and mind as you explore new experiences

- Repeat the Wheel of Life and the bonus practice often

We all know that the magic happens outside your comfort zone, but stepping out of the comfort requires a conscious decision to do so. Retreating after one bold leap won't yield the same results as making habit of living life beyond the confines of your current reality. It takes grit, courage and determination but the rewards are great. If you feel for Alana because you recognise yourself in her story, action is what will free you from this prison. You know the good stuff is beyond the comfort zone so get started and take one action today.

> *"I learned to always take on things I'd never done before. Growth and comfort do not coexist."*
>
> VIRGINIA ROMETTY, CEO OF IBM

Chapter 6: Fierce Independence
IS YOUR FIERCE INDEPENDENCE YOUR PRIMARY BUSINESS PRISON?

Your fear of failure has turned you into a control freak. You insist on doing everything yourself because you believe receiving support means you've failed, that you're weak or incompetent. You struggle to receive and you are stubborn. You resist getting help, thinking 'I can do it myself, I can handle it.' All the while, you're struggling and your unwillingness to let others support you has put a ceiling upon your growth. You resist change, often to your own detriment. You stick with what you know, even though you're totally capable of learning something new. It's difficult to see the bigger picture and look beyond your limited perspective. You pride yourself on being independent, like a badge of honour. You've got a tough facade, but you're totally vulnerable and that scares the shit out of you.

Here are some examples of how this prison shows up:

- Your fear of failure informs every decision you make and it's so deeply rooted you don't even see it

- You loathe the idea of being perceived as incompetent

- You say you're open-minded, but resist learning something new, even if it might be better

- You deny offers of help because 'you can handle it'

- You struggle silently, pushing through

- You have outbursts when it gets too much and the ones you love cop it

- You have heaps of manual processes because they're how you've always done it

- You refuse to admit you're struggling, because you always think maintaining power and control is a better option

- You're so damn capable and you forget others aren't exactly like you

- You need to control everrrrrrrything, even to the point that you're always the organiser for catch-ups and social events

- You like what you like and you feel like you know yourself really well now, but it's become a barrier

- You struggle to collaborate with others

- You are resistant, stubborn and reluctant to change how things are done

- It's hard to relate to others who aren't like you

- You think you know better than your mentors, and if you do hire a coach, you spend a lot of time telling them why their suggestions won't work

- You get irritated when technology changes

- When you're not supported, things are prone to fall apart

- You favour one-and-done or set-and-forget methods, because you don't want to keep having to incrementally improve or learn things

- You stick with systems and processes that are comfortable, unwilling to try new programs or software even if it's for your benefit

- You've got blinkers on and have a limited perspective on what is possible

Negative subconscious beliefs associated with this prison

- I can do it all by myself
- I don't need anyone's help
- I can just slog it out
- I'm tough
- I am not needy
- I like it like this
- Help is for other people who aren't like me
- It's my way or the highway
- I prefer the things I'm used to
- Getting help means I'm weak
- If I'm not perfect, I'm a failure
- My progress is slow

This prison is complex because you can create a profitable business while *inside* this prison. It can be tricky to recognise, like a blind spot. And even though you can create a reasonably successful business, it's inevitable that you'll eventually get stuck. In this prison, you reach your potential and stop dead in your tracks.

I know this one well. This one was **my** prison.

"We try to control what cannot be controlled, and we are never free as a result.
We dwell in stress and anxiety and the fear of the loss of control we never had in the first place."

CAROLINE MYSS

Prisoner story: Chenae (yep, that's me)

I like to be in control. I prefer to know how to do something before handing it over to my team. Why? I want to feel important. It's kinda ridiculous, right? I am the heart and soul of my business, yet my need for control saw me clinging to menial tasks, doing leverageable things that didn't match my role as CEO.

I'd experienced success doing things my way. I could see how my choices had served me really well, and I feared losing that success. I wanted to believe the previous decisions I'd made were good decisions so I didn't *really* push myself, either. We've all heard that Marianne Williamson quote about being afraid of our light; it's one of my favourites. Turns out, I was afraid of how much power I had, afraid of how amazing it could be. I'd done loads of personal development and knew myself really well. And yet, doing a lot of self-awareness work can mean that we become so fixed in an identity (for me it was my business identity) that expanding beyond that identity becomes the next uplevel, the next barrier to overcome.

There have been two times when I ran my business without any coaching or mentoring and they were the hardest times in my business. This became incredibly clear while on a business development retreat. Laura Elkaslassy (who wasn't yet my business mentor) shone a light on what she coined my 'DIY mindset' and how it was impacting my business growth. I desperately wanted to serve more clients and generate more profit, yet my fierce independence was slowing down systems that were designed to be efficient. No wonder I couldn't hit my income goal! In trying to do things *my way*, I was making it difficult. Thinking about how annoying

> *"The most dangerous phrase in business: 'We've always done it this way.'"*
>
> BEN ZIMMERMAN, FORBES

I must have been as a client (Laura's team does my bookkeeping) makes me cringe.

The next time I met with Laura was online to discuss my bookkeeping. She highlighted that I had a bunch of systems that weren't working optimally and she knew I wasn't reaching my goals. Knowing an uplevel was necessary, she gave me a challenge. She asked me to look at the big picture of my business and go beyond everything I knew, beyond what was comfortable, beyond everything that was familiar. She set me a seemingly simple task: *tell me what your business needs.*

It was hard. Really fucking hard. I can't even begin to explain how much I had to get out of my own damn way to think outside the box. It took me several days to even consider what was possible. After what felt like the longest week in history, I sent her my list. My list included a bunch of things I hadn't ever considered my business could offer. As a result of this process, I discovered that I had major blinkers on. My addiction to the familiar (under the guise of being fiercely independent) was suffocating my business. Urrrrgh, yuck.

Out of that process was the decision to implement Dubsado, a CRM tool in my business. Dubsado would amalgamate a bunch of my otherwise disconnected systems and streamline business operations. As I began the process, I began to see my blind spots. It was painful and frustrating; I didn't like not knowing what I was doing. I felt insecure. Not being able to do it myself was like being a three-year-old throwing a big fat tantrum because I couldn't get my way.

I was making everything hard for myself. If I wanted to make any progress, I was going to have to change my stubborn habits. I took a deep breath, asked for help, which meant eating a big old slice of humble pie. Et voilà! All my struggles melted away. I knew that what worked to get me to that point was not going to get me to the next level. And I wanted the next level. I was ready. Once I got it set up, Dubsado became a total game-changer and my business took off.

The belief underpinning my uplevel resistance was *I can do it all by myself.* I expected myself to be perfect, and when I wasn't, I felt like a failure. But I wasn't failing, I was **learning**.

JOURNAL ACTIVITY: REFLECTION QUESTIONS

As you read through my experience, make a note of anything that inspires you to free yourself from this prison. I've prepared a few journal prompts to deepen your reflection, based upon my own realisations and aha moments.

> *"To grow is to change, and to be perfect is to have changed often."*
>
> JOHN HENRY NEWMAN

- Do I ever expect myself to be perfect?

- If coaches need coaches and mentors need mentors, what do I need?

- Do I ever think I should be able to do it all myself?

- If I'm not perfect, what does that make me?

- Do I have the right support to see my blind spots?

- Is my reluctance to get help suffocating my business?

> *"People have a hard time letting go of their suffering. Out of a fear of the unknown, they prefer suffering that is familiar."*
>
> THICH NHAT HANH

AUDIO PRACTICE: REWRITING THE DOMINANT NARRATIVE

This audio practice is designed to challenge your self-sabotaging beliefs and start to make positive changes. When played on repeat, this audio can help you to rewire your neural pathways and create change. Listen here.

WHAT I LEARNED ABOUT MYSELF

- I was shitty at letting go
- I was chasing perfection instead of continuous improvement
- I need to practice what I preach because my service is my medicine
- When I can't see the forest for the trees, I need external input
- When I cling to things too tightly, it's hard to see the bigger picture
- I don't allow others to support me, because it feels uncomfortable
- Independence needs a healthy dash of humility
- When things are pointed out to me, it can be so simple
- I thrive when I have a mentor guiding me
- The teacher must also be the student

I was in the shadows, unwilling to be humble. Letting go of perfectionism is a journey for many of us. Now I say I am a *recovering perfectionist*, a term I first heard from my friend Claire Riley. This is why mentors need mentors and coaches need coaches.

WHICH OF THE FOLLOWING KEYS HOLD YOUR FREEDOM?

- Review all of your systems and processes with fresh eyes

- Be honest and identify what you need help with, and hire people with the expertise you need

"Perfectionism is a delusion that can rob one of a very successful, enriching life if not careful."

APRIL BRYAN

- Actually allow others help you

- Hire a team member

- Cowork with others regularly and discuss your challenges

- Journal about the stories you tell yourself about why you have to do it all yourself

- Uncover your blind spots and work on bringing them into view often

- Seek external input and feedback from credible peers and role models

- Reflect on the areas of your business that you DIY because you can, not because you should

- Recruit a systems specialist or a consultant

- Find 'letting go of control' meditations and apply them liberally

- If you don't have a VA, rectify that situation pronto

- Give up the badge of honour you carry about being independent

- Consult your peers for their input on how they would handle a decision you have to make

- Find role models who are fiercely independent and receive loads of support

- Visualise yourself feeling totally okay with imperfection

- Start acting like a CEO, not an apprentice or trainee

- Release your addiction to doing everything yourself

- Recruit someone to help you with your marketing, social media or both

- Do some energy work on your fear of failure

- Write down all of your strengths and weaknesses when it comes to your business

- Create an affirmation associated with humility and learning

- Delegate something *today* that you think you need to do yourself, but in truth you don't

- Explore one way you can do something you haven't allowed yourself to do before

- Work with a practitioner to release your need to control everything

- Do EFT on your perfectionism to loosen its grip

- Journal about your addiction to being in control

- Work with me

"We mourn because we cannot comprehend the swiftness of our own lifetime. Being alive is a precious gift - and no day will ever come again."

CAROLINE MYSS

I've included this chapter to show you that I really do get it. I'm just like you. I know what it's like and I'm now on the other side. I went from uplevel resistance to uplevel resilience and

Is Your Business a Prison?

I'm busier than ever with clients. They flow to me easily. I'm constantly learning, growing and expanding my comfort zone as I enjoy many forms of abundance. I feel supported. I feel liberated. I am thriving and there is not a prison cell in sight! The freedom is fucking fantastic. Get in touch if you'd like to do this together. I've literally been there, done that!

Where To From Here?

It's likely that you've seen yourself in one or more of the prisoners in these pages. You may resonate deeply with one specific prison, as if I've been peeking in your windows. Or maybe you can see yourself in a couple of different prisoner stories. Perhaps you can relate to them all. Regardless, I applaud you. The fact that you recognise yourself in *any* of these prisons is something to congratulate, because it takes courage to acknowledge the uncomfortable stuff. And for what it's worth, you're *totally* normal. I included these six prisons specifically because they're the ones I see the most.

If you've made it this far, it is my great hope that you've taken the time to explore each of the practices and tried a few different keys across each prison.

While each prison has a theme and a variety of keys, it takes a unique combination specific to you to unlock each layer. When you find the right key, you will feel it *click*. If you haven't already come to this conclusion, this book is not a one and done. Our beliefs have layers. Once you meet and release a belief, you may find a deeper layer in the days, weeks, months or even years to come. There is no formula, no blueprint, no step-by-step guide to reaching nirvana. It requires willingness.

I believe that our entrepreneurial freedom thrives with our ongoing attention, so if you regularly commit to exploring the prisons that resonate for you, you will reap the rewards. As you unlock more and more goodness, you will refine your business and embrace your version of entrepreneurial freedom at new heights and depths. Consider this my invitation to continue meeting your subconscious fears.

REVISITING THE CONTENT

As I said, this is not a one-and-done book. It's yours now, so use it as often as you need. Come back to your Wheel of Life every three to six months. Grab a buddy, set a reminder in your phone and review it together. Hold each other accountable. If you're having a shit day, come back to these pages and explore what belief might be informing your experiences, then apply the Micro Method liberally. Revisit your definition of entrepreneurial freedom and do some Heart Congruence.

I've put together a list of times when I think you should come back to this book. It's totally not exhaustive, but it's a start. Keep an eye out for the following, and if you notice it's happening, grab the book again.

- Sales slow down
- You're navigating a big uplevel
- Things feel hard or clunky
- Launching something new
- Implementing new software
- You feel disengaged
- Growing your team
- Your personal life is suffering at the hands of your business
- You're really stressed
- Business explodes and you can't keep up
- Closing down or discontinuing something
- Frustrated with a client
- Your business doesn't delight you
- Making a big business decision

I also recognise that this book alone might not be enough in some situations. If you want personalised support just like Hannah, Elle, and the other prisoners I've mentioned, please reach out or head to my website. The prisoners from these pages are now well and truly free and you can be too. The entrepreneurial freedom you desire is right there, waiting for you to claim it. Get in touch to find out how I can help.

My virtual door is open and regardless of whether you'd like to work with me further or not, I'd love to hear from you if you've made it this far. Tell me which prisoner(s) you relate to and why!

IN GRATITUDE

I'd like to close by expressing my heartfelt gratitude. Thank you so much for going on this journey with me. To my incredible clients whose stories are weaved through these pages, thank you. It's my absolute pleasure and privilege to serve you. You are brave and I am confident that your courage to free yourself is creating a ripple effect far beyond what your mind could possibly comprehend right now.

To wrap up, I'd like to leave you with a final quote from French author, journalist and philosopher Albert Camus. It feels both pertinent and inspiring.

Freedom is nothing but a chance to be better.

Thanks for reading.

xx

About the Author

Chenae Carey is an Intuitive Business Coach and Mentor for women-led businesses that make a difference. Established self-employed women who feel trapped by their business work with Chenae to achieve entrepreneurial freedom because they wholeheartedly believe that their business isn't meant to feel like a prison.

Chenae uses her Bachelor of Business and robust experience in the intuitive sciences to teach entrepreneurs how to confidently attract more clients, streamline their systems, align their energy to their goals and market effectively.